Mini Sweets

Mini Sweets

This edition published in 2012

LOVE FOOD is an imprint of Parragon Books Ltd

Parragon
Chartist House
15–17 Trim Street
Bath BA1 1HA, UK

www.parragon.com/lovefood

ISBN: 978-1-78186-381-7

Printed in China

Created and produced by Pene Parker and Becca Spry
Author and home economist: Sunil Vijayakar
Photographer: Karen Thomas

Notes for the reader

This book uses standard kitchen measuring spoons and cups. All spoon and cup measurements
are level unless otherwise indicated. Unless otherwise stated, milk is assumed to be whole, butter is
assumed to be unsalted, eggs are large, and individual fruits are medium.

The times given are only an approximate guide. Preparation times differ according to the techniques
used by different people and the cooking times may also vary from those given. Optional ingredients,
variations, or serving suggestions have not been included in the calculations.

Recipes using raw or very lightly cooked eggs should be avoided by infants, the elderly, pregnant
women, and people with weakened immune systems. Pregnant and breast-feeding women are
advised to avoid eating peanuts and peanut products. People with nut allergies should be aware that
some of the prepared ingredients used in the recipes in this book may contain nuts. Always check the
packaging before use.

Contents

Introduction

Everybody loves a sweet treat, and what could be more wonderful than being able to make, sample, and enjoy a variety of bite-size sweets that are easy to prepare, look terrific, and won't leave you feeling guilty about overindulging in our health-conscious society?

Ingredients

Chocolate

Dark, milk, and white chocolate and unsweetened cocoa powder are used in the recipes in this book. There are many brands and varieties of chocolate, and it is always worth buying the best you can afford. I recommend tasting it to see which you like the best — consider its appearance, aroma, flavor, texture, and aftertaste.

Semisweet dark chocolate contains at least 35 percent cocoa solids, and bittersweet dark chocolate can contain over 70 percent. The higher the percentage of cocoa solids, the richer the flavor. Milk chocolate usually contains at least 25 percent cocoa solids and tends to consist of cocoa butter, milk, sugar, and flavorings. White chocolate is made from cocoa butter, milk solids, sugar, flavorings such as vanilla, and emulsifiers such as lecithin.

Eggs

Eggs are a basic ingredient in baking. They serve many functions in sweets, providing structure, color, texture, flavor, and moisture. Use organic eggs if possible. Always check the date on the carton, and use eggs that are fresh. Do not use egg substitutes in place of fresh eggs, and always store your eggs in the refrigerator.

Flour

All-purpose flour is used in this book. It has a medium gluten content. It can be white or whole-wheat and does not contain a leavening agent. Don't substitute whole-wheat flour for white all-purpose flour in these recipes because it is heavier and more dense, so it will change the texture of the sweet. Self-rising flour has baking powder and salt added, so don't use it as a subsitute for all-purpose flour unless the recipes includes

baking powder and salt and you make adjustments; as a guide, 1 cup of self-rising flour contains 1½ teaspoons of baking powder and ½ teaspoon of salt.

Butter

All the recipes in this book use unsalted butter. This enables you to control the amount of salt in the sweet. Do not replace butter with margarine or butter substitutes, because this would affect the texture and flavor of the sweet.

Gelatin

This book uses both powdered and sheet gelatin. For powdered gelatin, scoop the powder into a measuring teaspoon so it is level with the spoon, then sprinkle it over your liquid. If specks remain on the surface of the liquid, gently stir them in using a teaspoon. For sheet gelatin, make sure the gelatin is completely submerged in the liquid. Let the gelatin soak for 10 minutes (it forms a sponge-like mixture).

Dried fruits and nuts

Dried fruits and nuts give sweets color, texture, and flavor. Many dried fruits and nuts are used in these recipes, including golden raisins, dried cranberries, dried apricots, ground almonds (almond meal), hazelnuts, cashew nuts, pistachio nuts, slivered almonds, walnuts, and pecans. Most of these can be substituted for one another in these recipes, if you prefer.

Sugar and spice

The spices and flavorings used in the recipes in this book include chili powder, ground ginger, ground cardamom seeds, vanilla extract, peppermint extract, and strawberry and raspberry flavorings. Make sure your spices are fresh. They should be stored in airtight containers once the jars or packages are opened.

Sugars add color, flavor, sweetness, and moisture. The recipes in this book use light brown, granulated, super-fine (you can make your own by processing the same amount of granulated sugar in a food processor for a minute), and confectioners' sugars and also syrups, such as light corn syrup and glucose syrup.

Always try to have these sugars and spices in your pantry at home.

Equipment

Here are some essential pieces of equipment for making mini sweets:

Heavy saucepans
Good, heavy saucepans in various sizes are crucial for working with sugar and chocolate, so they don't burn on the bottom of the pan.

Baking sheets and pans
You'll need nonstick baking sheets of various sizes, including ones that are 12 x 8 inches, 11 x 7 inches, and 8 inches square.

Heavy-duty metal baking sheets are best, because they don't buckle from the heat of the oven. Make sure you buy ones that fit in your oven.

You'll also need a loose-bottom cake pan measuring 8 inches square and another measuring 7 inches square, as well as a heavy 8-inch square baking pan and a 10-inch square baking pan for fudge.

Be sure to buy good-quality baking sheets and pans. It really is worth the extra money, because they will last a lifetime — as long as you take care of them properly.

Nonstick parchment paper
Nonstick parchment paper is invaluable for lining baking sheets and pans.

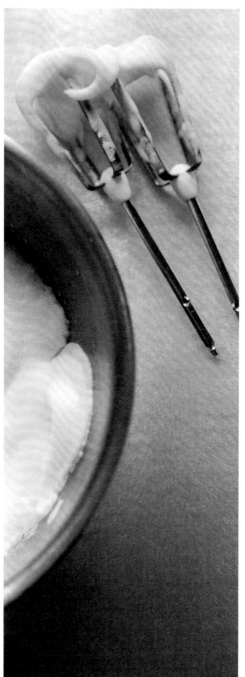

Candy thermometer

A candy thermometer is essential for cooking sugar mixtures to a particular desired temperature. It will read between 100°F and 400°F in small increments.

Make sure that the thermometer takes the temperature of the mixture in the pan and not of the bottom of the pan to get an accurate reading.

Electric mixer

The electric stand mixer is one of the most important tools for making sweets. It allows you to have your hands free while adding different ingredients or attending to other tasks as your ingredients are mixing.

Electric handheld mixer

The electric handheld mixer is crucial for beating, whipping, whisking, blending, and mixing ingredients for specific tasks, such as making macarons.

Food processor

The food processor is one of the most useful tools in the kitchen. It's terrific for chopping and grinding nuts as well as for blending mixtures.

Measuring cups and spoons

It is essential to have a standard set of kitchen measuring cups and measuring spoons as well as a large liquid measuring cup.

Microplane graters

Invest in stainless steel, razor-sharp graters in various sizes for different tasks, such as finely grating lemon rind and making chocolate curls.

Spatula

A heat-resistant rubber spatula is invaluable for stirring mixtures as they cook.

Kitchen timer

Kitchen timers come in all shapes and sizes. Use a timer that is easy to read. Always set the timer for the least amount of time called for in the recipe — you can always add more time, if needed.

Cooking techniques

Here are a few techniques used in the recipes in this book:

Melting chocolate

Put coarsely chopped or broken chocolate in a sturdy heatproof bowl that will fit snugly over a heavy saucepan, so that no heat or steam can escape. Bring the saucepan of water to a gentle simmer, then set the bowl over it and continue simmering over low heat until the chocolate has melted. Keep the water level in the pan at no more than 1 inch deep, and do not let the bottom of the bowl containing the chocolate touch the water or you may burn the chocolate. Once the chocolate has melted, use a rubber spatula to mix it until it is smooth. If you prefer to melt chocolate in a microwave, put the broken chocolate in a microwave-proof bowl and melt it on the lowest power in 30-second bursts. Stir with a rubber spatula after each burst.

Whisking eggs and egg whites

To whisk eggs to their full volume, it is best to first have them at room temperature. Use an electric stand mixer or handheld electric mixer with a bowl that is large enough for the eggs to triple in volume. Start with a medium speed and step it up to medium–high as the volume of the eggs increases in size. When whisking egg whites, it is very important that the bowl is clean with no trace of grease or fat, or they won't whisk properly. Egg whites can be frozen for up to three months. To defrost, allow them to come to room temperature before using.

Whipping cream

Chilled cream whips best, because it holds onto the air whipped into it better. Chill the bowl and beaters if you can before whipping the cream. Start whipping on a medium speed and watch carefully, because it can easily be overwhipped and get too firm. If this happens, you can rectify it by adding another couple of tablespoons of cream and whipping gently until it becomes smooth.

Chopping nuts

Chop nuts on a cutting board using a chef's knife or pulse them using a food processor.

Mini Fruit and Nut Sweets

Strawberry ripple marshmallows

Makes: 32
Prep: 40 minutes
Cook: 20 minutes
Set: 1 hour

Light and fluffy, these pretty cubes of sweetness and light will put a smile on everyone's face. They are equally good made with raspberry extract instead of strawberry.

a little sunflower oil, for greasing

cornstarch, for dusting

confectioners' sugar, sifted, for dusting

11 sheets of sheet gelatin (approximately ¾ ounce)

1½ cups water

1 tablespoon liquid glucose

2¼ cups superfine sugar

3 egg whites

1 teaspoon strawberry extract

2 teaspoons pink food coloring

1. Lightly brush a 12 x 8-inch baking pan with oil, then lightly dust it with cornstarch and sifted confectioners' sugar.

2. Put the gelatin into a small bowl and add ½ cup of water, making sure the gelatin is absorbed (see page 6). Set aside for 10 minutes.

3. Put the glucose, sugar, and remaining water into a medium, heavy saucepan. Bring to a boil, then reduce the heat and simmer for 15 minutes, or until the mixture reaches 260°F on a candy thermometer. Remove from the heat. Stir the gelatin mixture, then carefully spoon it into the pan; the syrup will bubble. Pour the syrup into a small bowl and stir.

4. Beat the egg whites in a large, clean mixing bowl until you have stiff, moist-looking peaks, then gradually beat in the hot syrup. The mixture will become shiny and start to thicken. Add the strawberry extract and beat for 5–10 minutes, until the mixture is stiff enough to hold its shape on the beaters.

5. Spoon the mixture into the prepared baking pan and smooth it, using a wet spatula. Sprinkle the food coloring over it and drag a small toothpick through it to create a marbled effect. Let set for 1 hour.

6. Loosen the marshmallow around the sides of the pan using a blunt knife, then invert it onto a board. Cut it into 32 squares, then lightly dust with cornstarch and sifted confectioners' sugar. Place on a wire rack to dry. Serve immediately.

Apple and apricot fruit gelatins

Makes: 30
Prep: 25 minutes
Cook: 10 minutes
Set: 3-4 hours

Called "jujubes" in many countries, these fruity cubes are refreshing and delicious. You can change the fruit flavor simply by using a different fruit juice and preserves.

2 cups apple juice

3 tablespoons powdered gelatin

2 cups superfine sugar

1½ cups apricot preserves

1. Put half the apple juice into a mixing bowl, then sprinkle the gelatin over the surface, making sure the powder is absorbed (see page 6). Set aside for 10 minutes.

2. Meanwhile, put the remaining apple juice and half the sugar into a heavy saucepan. Boil, stirring, for 5–6 minutes, or until the sugar has dissolved. Whisk in the preserves, then return to a boil and cook for 3–4 minutes, until the mixture is thick and syrupy. Whisk the gelatin into the syrup until it dissolves.

3. Pour the mixture through a fine-mesh strainer into a bowl. Transfer it to a 10 x 7-inch nonstick cake pan. Chill in the refrigerator for 3–4 hours, or until set.

4. Spread the remaining sugar over a large baking sheet. Cut the fruit gelatin into 30 squares and remove from the pan using a spatula. Toss in the sugar to coat just before serving. Serve or store in an airtight container in a cool, dry place for up to five days.

Raspberry coconut ice

Makes: 20
Prep: 30 minutes
Set: 3 hours

A no-cook sweet treat that is perfect to make with the kids. This is a wonderful gift when wrapped in cellophane bags or little gift boxes.

a little sunflower oil, for greasing

2½ cups confectioners' sugar, sifted, plus extra if needed

4½ cups dried coconut

1 (14-ounce) can sweetened condensed milk

1 teaspoon vanilla extract

½ cup raspberries

½ teaspoon pink food coloring

1 teaspoon raspberry extract

1. Lightly brush an 8-inch square baking pan with oil. Line the bottom with nonstick parchment paper.

2. Put half the sifted confectioners' sugar and half the coconut into one mixing bowl and put the other half into a second bowl. Stir the contents of each bowl, then make a well in the center.

3. Add half the condensed milk and half the vanilla to each of the coconut mixtures and stir. Press one of the mixtures into the prepared baking pan and level, using a spatula.

4. Put the raspberries into a blender and process to a puree. Push this through a strainer into a bowl to remove the seeds. Add the puree, food coloring, and raspberry extract to the remaining coconut mixture. Add more sifted confectioners' sugar if the mixture is too wet.

5. Spread the pink coconut ice over the white coconut layer, cover, then chill in the refrigerator for 3 hours, or until set.

6. Lift the coconut ice out of the pan, peel off the paper, and cut into 20 squares. Store in an airtight container in a cool, dry place for up to five days.

Mini toffee apples

Makes: 12
Prep: 25 minutes
Cook: 20–25 minutes

Nothing beats the crunch of a homemade toffee apple during a fall evening. Pack these miniature treats for an extra surprise around a campfire.

3 large red apples

juice of 1 lemon

½ cup superfine sugar

¾ cup water

1 tablespoon unsalted butter

a few drops of red food coloring

1. Put a bowl of iced water in the refrigerator. Using a melon scoop, scoop out 12 balls from the apples, making sure each ball has some red skin on it. Push a small toothpick into each ball through the red skin. Squeeze the lemon juice over the apple balls to prevent them from discoloring; set aside.

2. Put the sugar, water, and butter into a medium, heavy saucepan. Heat gently until the sugar has dissolved, tilting the pan to mix the ingredients together. Increase the heat and boil rapidly for 12–15 minutes, or until the mixture reaches 320°F on a candy thermometer and is deep golden. Turn off the heat, stir in the food coloring, and let the bubbles subside.

3. Remove the bowl of iced water from the refrigerator. Working as quickly as possible, dip the apples into the toffee, one at a time, rotating them a few times to get an even coating, then drop them into the iced water for 30 seconds. Serve immediately.

Pistachio and apricot nougat

Makes: 16
Prep: 30 minutes
Cook: 15 minutes
Set: 8–10 hours

A confection made from boiled honey and sugar syrup mixed with beaten egg white, nuts, and dried fruit. It is associated with the French town of Montélimar, where it has been made since the eighteenth century. Enjoy it as an after dinner sweet with coffee, crumble it over ice cream, or use it in desserts.

edible rice paper

1¼ cups superfine sugar

½ cup liquid glucose

⅓ cup honey

2 tablespoons water

a pinch of salt

1 egg white

½ teaspoon vanilla extract

4 tablespoons unsalted butter, softened and diced

⅓ cup coarsely chopped pistachio nuts

⅓ cup finely chopped dried apricots

1. Line a 7-inch square baking pan with plastic wrap, leaving an overhang. Line the bottom with edible rice paper.

2. Put the sugar, glucose, honey, water, and salt into a heavy saucepan. Heat gently until the sugar has dissolved, tilting the pan to mix the ingredients together. Increase the heat and boil for 8 minutes, or until the mixture reaches 250°F on a candy thermometer.

3. Put the egg white into a freestanding mixer, or use a handheld mixer, and beat until firm. Gradually pour in one-quarter of the hot syrup in a thin stream while still beating the egg. Continue beating for 5 minutes, until the mixture is stiff enough to hold its shape on the beaters.

4. Put the pan containing the remaining syrup over gentle heat for 2 minutes, or until the mixture reaches 290°F on a candy thermometer. Gradually pour the syrup over the egg mixture while beating.

5. Add the vanilla and butter and beat for an additional 5 minutes. Add the pistachios and apricots and stir.

6. Pour the mixture into the prepared baking pan and level, using a spatula. Cover with edible rice paper and chill in the refrigerator for 8–10 hours, or until fairly firm.

7. Lift the nougat out of the pan and cut into 16 squares. Serve or store in an airtight container in the refrigerator for up to five days.

Peanut butter and chocolate candy balls

Makes: 36
Prep: 25 minutes
Cook: 5 minutes
Set: 4–6 hours

This recipe uses semisweet chocolate to coat the peanut candy balls, but, if you prefer, you can use milk or white chocolate, or a mixture of the three.

1 cup smooth peanut butter

4 tablespoons unsalted butter

¾ cup crisp rice cereal

1⅔ cups confectioners' sugar

8 ounces semisweet chocolate, coarsely chopped

1. Line two baking sheets with nonstick parchment paper. Melt the peanut butter and butter together in a heavy saucepan.

2. Put the rice cereal and confectioners' sugar into a large mixing bowl. Pour in the melted butter mixture, then stir. When cool enough to handle, using the palms of your hands, roll the mixture into 1-inch balls, then put them on the prepared baking sheets and chill in the refrigerator for 3–4 hours, or until firm.

3. Put the chocolate in a heatproof bowl, set the bowl over a saucepan of gently simmering water, and heat until melted.

4. Using a teaspoon, dip the balls into the chocolate, one by one, making sure they are covered completely, then lift them out and return them to the baking sheets. Chill in the refrigerator for 1–2 hours, or until set. Serve or store in an airtight container in the refrigerator for up to five days.

Sea-salted pecan candies

Makes: 12
Prep: 15 minutes
Cook: 10–15 minutes
Set: 10 minutes

You can replace the pecans with walnuts, whole peeled almonds, or cashew nuts, if you prefer.

½ cup pecans

1½ cups superfine sugar

¾ cup water

2 teaspoons sea salt

1. Preheat the oven to 325°F. Put the pecans on a baking sheet and toast them in the preheated oven for 3–4 minutes, or until golden, shaking them halfway through. Divide the nuts between the cups of a 12-cup silicone miniature muffin pan.

2. Put the sugar and water into a heavy saucepan. Heat gently, tilting the pan to mix together the ingredients, until the sugar has dissolved and the mixture reaches an even light brown color. Continue cooking until it is a slightly deeper brown, watching it carefully so it doesn't burn. Sprinkle with the sea salt and transfer to a jug for easy pouring.

3. Quickly pour the mixture into the muffin cups. Let cool for 10 minutes, until the candies set and harden. Invert the candies out of the cups. Store in an airtight container in a cool, dry place for up to five days.

Mini Toffee and Fudge Sweets

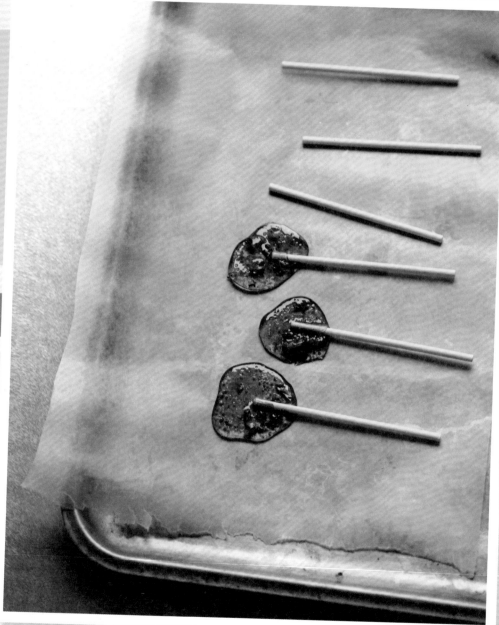

Toffee popcorn

Makes: about 25 cups
Prep: 15 minutes
Cook: 5–10 minutes

This popcorn is fun to make as a treat for children's birthday parties. For adults, sprinkle on a little cayenne pepper to get a sweet and spicy kick.

2 tablespoons unsalted butter

½ cup popping corn

TOFFEE COATING

3 tablespoons unsalted butter

¼ cup firmly packed dark brown sugar

2 tablespoons light corn syrup

1. Melt the butter in a large, heavy saucepan. Add the popping corn and swirl the pan to coat the corn evenly.

2. Cover the pan with a tight-fitting lid, reduce the heat to low, and let the corn start popping. Shake the pan a couple of times to move the unpopped pieces to the bottom. As soon as the popping stops, take the pan off the heat and let stand, covered.

3. For the toffee coating, melt the butter in a medium, heavy saucepan. Add the sugar and syrup and cook over high heat, stirring, for 1–2 minutes, or until the sugar has dissolved.

4. Pour the toffee coating over the popped corn, replace the lid on the pan, and shake well. Let cool slightly, then serve immediately.

Honeycomb brittle

Makes: about 20
Prep: 15 minutes
Cook: 10–15 minutes
Set: 5 minutes

Known as hokey-pokey in Australia, this light and crunchy brittle is perfect broken into bite-size pieces or crushed over ice cream.

a little sunflower oil, for greasing

1 cup superfine sugar

½ cup light corn syrup

1 stick unsalted butter, diced

2 teaspoons baking soda

1. Lightly brush an 8-inch square baking pan with oil.

2. Put the sugar, syrup, and butter into a large, heavy saucepan. Heat gently until the sugar has dissolved, tilting the pan to mix the ingredients together. Increase the heat and boil rapidly for 4–5 minutes, or until the mixture turns a light golden color.

3. Add the baking soda and stir for a few seconds; be careful because the mixture will expand and bubble.

4. Pour the mixture into the prepared baking pan. Let cool for 5 minutes, or until set. Break the brittle into shards. Store in an airtight container in a cool, dry place for up to two weeks.

Sesame, marshmallow, and cranberry squares

Makes: 20
Prep: 15 minutes
Cook: 20 minutes

These are best baked in advance. They make a great afternoon treat or lunch box filler.

1⅔ cup rolled oats

⅓ cup sesame seeds

3 tablespoons firmly packed light brown sugar

⅔ cup miniature marshmallows

½ cup dried cranberries

½ cup honey

⅓ cup sunflower oil, plus extra for greasing

a few drops of vanilla extract

1. Preheat the oven to 325°F. Lightly brush a 11 x 7-inch baking pan with oil. Line the bottom with nonstick parchment paper.

2. Put the oats, sesame seeds, sugar, marshmallows, and cranberries into a mixing bowl and stir. Make a well in the center, add the honey, oil, and vanilla extract, then stir again.

3. Press the mixture into the prepared baking pan and level, using a metal spoon. Bake in the preheated oven for 20 minutes, or until golden and bubbling.

4. Let cool in the pan for 10 minutes, then cut into small squares. Let cool completely before turning out of the pan. Store in an airtight container in a cool, dry place for up to two days.

Cashew nut brittle

Makes: about 20
Prep: 15 minutes
Cook: 25-30 minutes

This is a wonderful, buttery brittle that is easy to make and wows everyone! You could use roasted peanuts instead of cashew nuts, if you prefer.

1¼ cups roasted, salted cashew nuts

1¾ cups superfine sugar

¼ teaspoon cream of tartar

1 cup water

1 tablespoon unsalted butter

1. Line an 8-inch square baking pan with nonstick parchment paper.

2. Spread the cashew nuts in the baking pan in a thin, even layer.

3. Put the sugar, cream of tartar, and water into a heavy saucepan. Bring to a gentle boil over medium heat, stirring all the time.

4. Reduce the heat to low and simmer for 20–25 minutes without stirring, until the mixture reaches 290°F on a candy thermometer. Stir in the butter, then carefully drizzle the caramel over the nuts. Let cool completely.

5. Break the brittle into shards. Serve or store in an airtight container in a cool, dry place for up to two days.

Fruit and nut brittle

Makes: 12
Prep: 25 minutes
Cook: 25-30 minutes
Set: 5 minutes

These individual candy-and-nut "lollipops" have an exotic flavor and texture that will impress kids and adults alike.

1¼ cups superfine sugar

¼ teaspoon cream of tartar

⅔ cup water

2 tablespoons finely chopped pistachio nuts

1 tablespoon finely chopped dried apricots

1 tablespoon dried rose petals (optional)

a large pinch of ground cardamom seeds

1. Line a large baking sheet with parchment paper. Put 12 lollipop sticks on the prepared sheet, spaced well apart.

2. Put the sugar, cream of tartar, and water into a heavy saucepan. Bring to a gentle boil over medium heat, stirring all the time.

3. Reduce the heat to low and simmer for 20–25 minutes without stirring, until the mixture reaches 290°F on a candy thermometer.

4. Remove the pan from the heat and stir in the pistachios, apricots, rose petals, if using, and ground cardamom.

5. Working quickly, spoon a large teaspoon of the syrup onto one end of each lollipop stick. Let set for 5 minutes, until hard. Store in an airtight container in a cool, dry place for up to two weeks.

Vanilla fudge

Makes: 16
Prep: 15 minutes
Cook: 10–15 minutes
Set: 1 hour

Just five simple ingredients and you can make the creamiest vanilla fudge ever. A guaranteed hit! Be careful when you stir the fudge, because the mixture gets very hot.

a little sunflower oil, for greasing

2¼ cups superfine sugar

6 tablespoons unsalted butter

⅔ cup whole milk

⅔ cup evaporated milk

2 teaspoons vanilla extract

1. Lightly brush an 8-inch square baking pan with oil. Line the bottom with nonstick parchment paper.

2. Put the sugar, butter, milk, and evaporated milk into a heavy saucepan. Heat gently, stirring, until the sugar has dissolved.

3. Increase the heat and boil for 12–15 minutes, or until the mixture reaches 240°F on a candy thermometer (if you don't have a candy thermometer, spoon a little of the syrup into some iced water; it will form a soft ball when it is ready). As the temperature rises, stir the fudge occasionally so the sugar doesn't stick and burn.

4. Remove the pan from the heat, add the vanilla, and beat, using a wooden spoon, until thickened.

5. Pour the mixture into the prepared baking pan and smooth the surface, using a spatula. Let cool for 1 hour, or until set.

6. Lift the fudge out of the pan, peel off the paper, and cut into small squares. Store in an airtight container in a cool, dry place for up to two weeks.

Indulgent whiskey fudge

Makes: 16
Prep: 15 minutes
Cook: 10–15 minutes
Set 2–3 hours

If you are a chocolate and whiskey lover, this is the perfect edible treat. You can use a good brandy instead of whiskey, if you prefer.

a little sunflower oil, for greasing

1 cup firmly packed brown sugar

1 stick unsalted butter, diced

1 (14-ounce) can sweetened condensed milk

2 tablespoons glucose syrup

¼ cup walnut pieces

6 ounces semisweet chocolate, coarsely chopped

¼ cup whiskey

1. Lightly brush an 8-inch square baking pan with oil. Line it with nonstick parchment paper, snipping diagonally into the corners, then pressing the paper into the pan so that the bottom and sides are lined

2. Put the sugar, butter, condensed milk, and glucose into a heavy saucepan. Heat gently, stirring, until the sugar has dissolved. Increase the heat and boil for 12–15 minutes, or until the mixture reaches 240°F on a candy thermometer (if you don't have a candy thermometer, spoon a little syrup into some iced water; it will form a soft ball when it is ready). As the temperature rises, stir the fudge occasionally so the sugar doesn't burn.

3. Meanwhile, preheat the broiler to medium–hot. Put the walnuts in a baking sheet and toast them under the broiler for 2–3 minutes, or until browned. Coarsely chop them.

4. Remove the fudge from the heat. Add the chocolate and whiskey and stir together until the chocolate has melted and the mixture is smooth.

5. Pour the mixture into the prepared baking pan, smooth the surface, using a spatula, and sprinkle the walnuts over it. Let cool for 1 hour. Cover with plastic wrap, then chill in the refrigerator for 1–2 hours, or until firm. Lift the fudge out of the pan, peel off the paper, and cut into small squares. Store in an airtight container in a cool, dry place for up to two weeks.

Chocolate Pretzel Fudge Squares

Makes: 16
Prep: 15 minutes
Cook: 8–10 minutes
Set: 2–3 hours

These are so easy to make. The salty pretzels counteract the rich sweetness of the chocolate and condensed milk.

1 (7-ounce) package mini pretzels

a little sunflower oil, for greasing

2 tablespoons unsalted butter, diced

1¾ cups milk chocolate chips

1 (14-ounce) can sweetened condensed milk

1 teaspoon vanilla extract

1. Coarsely chop one-third of the pretzels.

2. Lightly brush a 10-inch square baking pan with oil. Line it with nonstick parchment paper, snipping diagonally into the corners, then pressing the paper into the pan so that the bottom and sides are lined and there is a 2-inch overhang on all sides.

3. Put the butter, chocolate chips, condensed milk, and vanilla in a heatproof bowl, set the bowl over a saucepan of gently simmering water, and heat, stirring occasionally, for 8–10 minutes, or until the chocolate has just melted and the mixture is smooth and warm but not hot. Remove from the heat and stir in the chopped pretzels.

4. Pour the mixture into the prepared pan, smooth the surface, using a spatula, and push in the whole pretzels. Let cool for 1 hour. Cover with plastic wrap, then chill in the refrigerator for 1–2 hours, or until firm.

5. Lift the fudge out of the pan, peel off the paper, and cut it into small squares. Store in an airtight container in a cool, dry place for up to two weeks.

Mini Chocolate Sweets

Chocolate-coated candied orange rind

Makes: 36
Prep: 55 minutes
Cook: 1 hour
Set: 2–4 hours

Strips of candied orange rind dipped in dark chocolate make an elegant gift. Alternatively, serve them with coffee after dinner.

3 large navel oranges

1 cup sugar

8 ounces semisweet chocolate, coarsely chopped

1. Using a sharp knife, cut the rind off the oranges, then remove the white pith from the rind. Slice the rind into thirty-six 2½ x ½-inch strips, discarding any you don't need.

2. Bring a small saucepan of water to a boil, then add the orange rind and simmer for 10 minutes. Drain, then rinse under cold running water. Pour more water into the pan and bring it to a boil again, then return the rind to the pan and simmer for an additional 10 minutes. Repeat this process one more time.

3. Put the sugar and 1 cup of water into a heavy saucepan. Bring it to a boil and simmer gently, stirring, for 5 minutes, or until the sugar has dissolved and the mixture has reduced a little in volume. Add the orange rind and continue simmering for 15 minutes. Transfer the candied peel to a wire rack and let cool for 1–2 hours or overnight.

4. Line a baking sheet with nonstick parchment paper. Put the chocolate in a heatproof bowl, set the bowl over a saucepan of gently simmering water, and heat until melted.

5. Dip one-third of the length of each candied orange strip in the chocolate and place it on the prepared baking sheet. Let cool for 1–2 hours, or until set. Store in an airtight container in a cool, dry place for up to five days.

Salted caramel and chocolate bites

Makes: 20
Prep: 30 minutes
Cook: 35-40 minutes

Sea salt and caramel is a classic combination, and here it is enhanced by the addition of walnuts.

a little sunflower oil, for greasing

8 ounces semisweet chocolate, coarsely chopped

1¼ sticks unsalted butter

2 eggs

¾ cup firmly packed light brown sugar

½ cup all-purpose flour

1 teaspoon baking powder

½ cup coarsely chopped walnuts

⅓ cup dulce de leche (caramel sauce)

1 tablespoon sea salt

1. Preheat the oven to 325°F. Lightly brush an 8-inch square baking pan with oil. Line it with nonstick parchment paper, snipping diagonally into the corners, then pressing the paper into the pan so that the bottom and sides are lined.

2. Put 2 ounces of the chocolate and all the butter in a heatproof bowl, set the bowl over a saucepan of gently simmering water, and heat until melted, stirring from time to time.

3. Put the eggs and sugar into a mixing bowl, then sift in the flour and baking powder. Stir in the melted chocolate mixture and whisk together until blended. Add the walnuts and remaining chocolate and stir together. Pour the mixture into the prepared baking pan and smooth the surface, using a spatula.

4. Put the dulce de leche into a small mixing bowl and beat, then swirl it through the chocolate mixture using a fork. Sprinkle with the sea salt and bake in the preheated oven for 30-35 minutes, or until the cake begins to shrink slightly from the sides of the pan. Let cool for 1 hour.

5. Lift the cake out of the pan, peel off the paper, and cut it into small squares. Store in an airtight container in a cool, dry place for up to two days.

White and dark chocolate-dipped strawberries

Makes: 24
Prep: 10 minutes
Cook: 3-4 minutes
Set: 1 hour

Chocolate always makes a sweet mouthful special, and in this fun, party treat it is paired with delicious strawberries. Prepare it several hours before you plan to serve it, if you prefer.

4 ounces semisweet chocolate, coarsely chopped

4 ounces white chocolate, coarsely chopped

24 large strawberries

1. Line a baking sheet with nonstick parchment paper. Put the semisweet chocolate and white chocolate into two separate heatproof bowls, set the bowls over two saucepans of gently simmering water, and heat until melted.

2. Dip the pointed end of each strawberry into one of the melted chocolates and transfer it to the prepared baking sheet. Let cool for 1 hour, or until set.

3. Put each strawberry in a liqueur glass or on a plate and serve immediately.

Mini cranberry and ginger florentines

Makes: 48
Prep: 30 minutes
Cook: 15–20 minutes
Set: 2 hours

These crispy and chewy bites are an Italian classic and make a marvelous present.

⅓ cup firmly packed brown sugar

¼ cup honey

1 stick unsalted butter, plus extra for greasing

¾ cup dried coconut

¾ cup slivered almonds

1 tablespoon finely chopped candied peel

1 tablespoon finely chopped preserved ginger

⅔ cup dried cranberries

½ cup all-purpose flour, plus extra for dusting

8 ounces semisweet chocolate, coarsely chopped

1. Preheat the oven to 350°F. Using butter, lightly grease four 12-cup miniature muffin pans (the bottom of each cup should be ¾ inch in diameter), then lightly dust them with flour.

2. Put the sugar, honey, and butter into a heavy saucepan. Heat gently, stirring, until the sugar has dissolved, tilting the pan to mix together the ingredients. Stir in the coconut, almonds, candied peel, preserved ginger, cranberries, and flour.

3. Put small teaspoons of the batter into the prepared muffin pans. Bake in the preheated oven for 10–12 minutes, or until golden brown. Let cool in the pans for 1 hour. Using a spatula, transfer to a wire rack until firm.

4. Meanwhile, put the chocolate in a heatproof bowl, set the bowl over a saucepan of gently simmering water, and heat until melted.

5. Dip each florentine into the melted chocolate so the bottom is covered. Place on a wire rack, chocolate side up, and let set for 1 hour. Store in an airtight container in a cool, dry place for up to two days.

Chocolate meringue kisses

Makes: 40
Prep: 40 minutes
Cook: 50 minutes
Set: 2 hours

Elegant little "kisses" of melt-in-the-mouth meringue dipped in chocolate, these make a very good canapé or gift.

3 egg whites

1 teaspoon raspberry vinegar

¾ cup superfine sugar

1 teaspoon cornstarch

2 tablespoons unsweetened cocoa powder, sifted

8 ounces semisweet chocolate, coarsely chopped

1. Preheat the oven to 325°F. Line three baking sheets with nonstick parchment paper.

2. Whisk the egg whites in a large, clean mixing bowl until you have stiff, moist-looking peaks. Gradually whisk in the vinegar and sugar, a tablespoonful at a time, until thick and glossy. Using a large metal spoon, gently fold in the cornstarch and cocoa.

3. Spoon the mixture into a pastry bag fitted with a large star tip and pipe forty 1-inch "kisses" onto the prepared baking sheets.

4. Put the sheets in the preheated oven, then immediately turn the heat down to 250°F. Bake for 45 minutes, or until crisp on the outside. Transfer the meringues to a wire rack, still on the paper, and let cool for 1 hour, then peel off the paper.

5. Meanwhile, put the chocolate in a heatproof bowl, set the bowl over a saucepan of gently simmering water, and heat until melted.

6. Line the baking sheets with more parchment paper. Dip the bottoms of the meringue kisses in the melted chocolate and place them, chocolate side up, on the prepared baking sheets. Let set for 1 hour. Store in an airtight container in a cool, dry place for up to two weeks.

Nutty peppermint bark

Makes: about 25
Prep: 20 minutes
Cook: 3–4 minutes
Set: 30 minutes

Kids and adults alike will love this treat. If you can't get hold of peppermint candy canes, substitute them with any mint candy.

7 ounces red-and-white striped peppermint candy canes, broken into pieces

1 pound white chocolate, coarsely chopped

1 cup chopped mixed nuts

1. Line a 12 x 8-inch baking sheet with nonstick parchment paper.

2. Put the broken candy into a large plastic food bag and seal tightly. Using a rolling pin, bash the bag until the candy is crushed into small pieces.

3. Put the chocolate in a heatproof bowl, set the bowl over a saucepan of gently simmering water, and heat until melted. Remove from the heat and stir in three-quarters of the candy.

4. Pour the mixture into the prepared baking sheet, smooth the surface, using a spatula, and sprinkle over the chopped nuts and remaining candy. Press down very slightly to make sure they stick. Cover with plastic wrap and chill in the refrigerator for 30 minutes, or until firm.

5. Break the peppermint bark into small, uneven pieces. Store in an airtight container in a cool, dry place for up to two weeks.

Mini chocolate-dipped donuts

Makes: 50
Prep: 30 minutes
Cook: 1½–2 hours

These mini donuts can be served dusted with superfine sugar instead of being dipped in chocolate, if you prefer.

4 cups all-purpose flour, plus extra for dusting

2 tablespoons plus 1 teaspoon baking powder

½ cup superfine sugar

2 eggs

2 tablespoons sunflower oil, plus extra for deep frying

1 cup milk

4 ounces semisweet chocolate, coarsely chopped

1. Lightly dust a work surface with flour. Sift the flour and baking powder into a large mixing bowl. Add the sugar and stir.

2. Put the eggs, 2 tablespoons of oil, and the milk into a separate mixing bowl and beat together lightly, then pour this into the flour mixture. Using a wooden spoon, work the ingredients into a smooth ball, then invert it onto the floured work surface.

3. Using a floured rolling pin, roll the dough out to a thickness of just over ½ inch. Flour a 1½-inch and a ½-inch round cutter. Use the larger cutter to cut out circles of dough, then use the smaller one to cut out the centers. Reroll the trimmings to make more donuts.

4. Heat the oil for deep frying in a deep saucepan until it reaches 350°F, or until a small piece of bread dropped in sizzles immediately.

5. Line a plate with paper towels. Carefully lower two to three donut rings into the hot oil and cook for 3–4 minutes, until golden and cooked through. Transfer to the paper towel-lined plate to drain and cool. Continue cooking in batches of this size until all the donuts are ready.

6. Put the chocolate in a heatproof bowl, set the bowl over a saucepan of gently simmering water, and heat until melted. Dip the top of the donuts in the melted chocolate and transfer to a wire rack for 1 hour. Serve immediately.

Chocolate moustaches

Makes: 6
Prep: 10 minutes
Cook: 3-4 minutes
Set: 1 hour

For the genteel gentleman or big kid, here's a dark and delicious moustache lollipop. These are loads of fun to serve at parties — make sure you have a camera to make the most of a great photo opportunity!

8 ounces semisweet chocolate, coarsely chopped

1. Put the chocolate in a heatproof bowl, set the bowl over a saucepan of gently simmering water, and heat until melted. Let cool for a few minutes.

2. Pour the melted chocolate into six x 3 fluid ounce moustache molds.

3. Push a lollipop stick firmly into each moustache. Chill in the refrigerator for 1 hour, or until set. Gently invert out of the molds. Store in an airtight container in a cool, dry place for up to two weeks.

Mini After Dinner Sweets

Peppermint creams

Makes: 25
Prep: 30 minutes
Set: 25 hours

The pretty and tasty peppermint cream is an old-fashioned favorite. It's a refreshing choice for an after dinner treat.

1 extra-large egg white

2½ cups confectioners' sugar, sifted, plus extra for dipping if needed

a few drops of peppermint extract

a few drops of green food coloring

4 ounces semisweet chocolate, coarsely chopped

1. Line a baking sheet with nonstick parchment paper.

2. Lightly whisk the egg white in a large, clean mixing bowl until it is frothy but still translucent.

3. Add the sifted confectioners' sugar to the egg white and stir, using a wooden spoon, until the mixture is stiff. Knead in the peppermint extract and food coloring.

4. Using the palms of your hands, roll the mixture into walnut-size balls and place them on the prepared baking sheet. Use a fork to flatten them; if it sticks to them, dip it in confectioners' sugar before pressing. Put the creams in the refrigerator to set for 24 hours.

5. Put the chocolate in a heatproof bowl, set the bowl over a saucepan of gently simmering water, and heat until melted. Dip the creams halfway in the chocolate and return to the baking sheet for 1 hour, or until set. Store in an airtight container in the refrigerator for up to five days.

Dark chocolate and amaretto truffles

Makes: 12
Prep: 30 minutes
Soak: 6–8 hours
Cook: 5–10 minutes
Set: 1–2 hours

These delectable morsels are so easy to make and look really glamorous! Use any liqueur instead of the amaretto, if you prefer.

¼ cup amaretto liqueur

⅓ cup golden raisins

4 ounces semisweet chocolate, coarsely chopped

2 tablespoons heavy cream

2½ ounces of store-bought chocolate cake or brownie, crumbled

1 cup hazelnuts

¼ cup chocolate sprinkles, to decorate

1. Put the amaretto and golden raisins into a small mixing bowl, cover, and let soak for 6–8 hours. Line a baking sheet with nonstick parchment paper.

2. Transfer the amaretto mixture to a food processor and process until pureed.

3. Put the chocolate and cream in a heatproof bowl, set the bowl over a saucepan of gently simmering water, and heat until melted. Remove from the heat, add the amaretto puree and chocolate cake, and stir well.

4. When cool enough to handle, using the palms of your hands, roll the mixture into truffle-size balls and place on the prepared baking sheet.

5. Preheat the broiler to medium. Put the hazelnuts on a second baking sheet and toast them under the broiler for 2–3 minutes, or until browned, shaking them halfway through. Finely chop them.

6. Spread the chocolate sprinkles onto one plate and the hazelnuts onto another. Roll half the truffles in the chocolate and half in the hazelnuts. Return to the baking sheet, cover with nonstick parchment paper, and chill in the refrigerator for 1–2 hours, or until firm. Store in an airtight container in the refrigerator for up to five days.

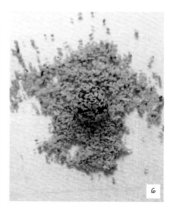

Lemon and white chocolate creams

Makes: 12
Prep: 40 minutes
Cook: 5–10 minutes
Set: 13–18 hours

For an Asian twist on these decadent truffles, add a large pinch each of ground cardamom seeds and star anise to the cream-and-chocolate mixture.

10 ounces white chocolate, coarsely chopped

2 tablespoons heavy cream

finely grated rind of 1 lemon

2 tablespoons limoncello

4 tablespoons unsalted butter, softened and diced

3 tablespoons finely chopped pistachio nuts

1. Put 4 ounces of the chocolate and all the cream in a heatproof bowl, set the bowl over a saucepan of gently simmering water, and heat until melted.

2. Remove from the heat, add the lemon rind, limoncello, and butter, and beat for 3–4 minutes, or until thickened. Transfer to an airtight container and chill in the refrigerator for 6–8 hours, or until firm.

3. Line a baking sheet with nonstick parchment paper. Scoop teaspoonfuls of the mixture and, using the palms of your hands, roll them into truffle-size balls. Place the balls on the prepared baking sheet, cover with plastic wrap, and freeze for 6–8 hours.

4. Put the remaining chocolate in a heatproof bowl, set the bowl over a saucepan of gently simmering water, and heat until melted. Using two forks, dip each truffle into the chocolate to coat evenly. Return them to the prepared baking sheet, sprinkle the pistachios over them, and chill in the refrigerator for 1–2 hours, or until firm. Store in an airtight container in the refrigerator for up to five days.

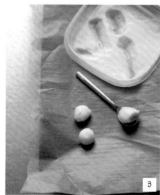

Espresso truffles

Makes: 12
Prep: 40 minutes
Cook: 5–10 minutes
Set: 13–18 hours

For a twist on these coffee truffles, simply replace the coffee with Baileys Irish Cream liqueur or any orange-flavored liqueur, such as Grand Marnier or Cointreau.

10 ounces semisweet chocolate, coarsely chopped

2 tablespoons heavy cream

1 tablespoon strong espresso coffee, cooled

2 tablespoons coffee liqueur

4 tablespoons unsalted butter, softened and diced

edible gold leaf, to decorate (optional)

1. Put 4 ounces of the chocolate and all the cream in a heatproof bowl, set the bowl over a saucepan of gently simmering water, and heat until melted.

2. Remove from the heat, add the espresso, coffee liqueur, and butter, and beat for 3–4 minutes, or until thickened. Transfer to an airtight container and chill in the refrigerator for 6–8 hours, or until firm.

3. Line a baking sheet with nonstick parchment paper. Scoop teaspoonfuls of the mixture and, using the palms of your hands, roll them into truffle-size balls. Place the balls on the prepared baking sheet, cover with plastic wrap, and freeze for 6–8 hours.

4. Put the remaining chocolate in a heatproof bowl, set the bowl over a saucepan of gently simmering water, and heat until melted. Using two forks, dip each truffle into the chocolate to coat evenly. Return them to the prepared baking sheet and chill in the refrigerator for 1–2 hours, or until firm. Top each truffle with edible gold leaf to decorate, if desired. Store in an airtight container in the refrigerator for up to five days.

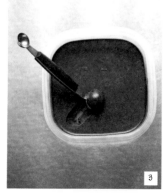

Chili and cardamom chocolate thins

Makes: 40
Prep: 30 minutes
Cook: 5–10 minutes
Set: 1–2 hours

These simple treats are perfect for kids to make. They're ideal for putting into a pretty box and giving as a present, too.

CHILI DARK CHOCOLATE THINS

8 ounces semisweet chocolate, coarsely chopped

a large pinch of hot chili powder

edible glitter, to decorate

CARDAMOM WHITE CHOCOLATE THINS

8 ounces white chocolate, coarsely chopped

½ teaspoon cardamom seeds, crushed

3 tablespoons finely chopped pistachio nuts, plus extra to decorate

edible glitter, to decorate

1. Line four baking sheets with nonstick parchment paper.

2. For the chili dark chocolate thins, put the semisweet chocolate in a heatproof bowl, set the bowl over a saucepan of gently simmering water, and heat until melted. Remove from the heat and stir in the chili powder.

3. Drop teaspoons of the chocolate mixture onto two of the prepared baking sheets. Sprinkle with a little edible glitter before the chocolate sets. Let set in a cool place, but not in the refrigerator, for 1–2 hours.

4. For the cardamom white chocolate thins, put the white chocolate in a heatproof bowl, set the bowl over a saucepan of gently simmering water, and heat until melted. Remove from the heat and stir in the cardamom and pistachios.

5. Drop teaspoonfuls of the white chocolate mixture onto the remaining two prepared baking sheets. Sprinkle the remaining chopped pistachios and a little edible glitter over them before the chocolate sets. Let set in a cool place, but not in the refrigerator, for 1–2 hours. Store in an airtight container in a cool, dry place for up to five days.

Mini macarons

Makes: 20
Prep: 1¼ hours
Cook: 30–35 minutes
Set: 1–2 hours

Measure your ingredients carefully when making these delectable macarons, because it is crucial to get the proportions right.

1 cup confectioners' sugar, sifted

1⅓ cups almond meal
(ground almonds)

2 extra-large egg whites

½ cup superfine sugar

3 tablespoons water

a few drops of pink food
coloring

BUTTERCREAM

1¼ sticks unsalted butter,
softened

2¼ cups confectioners' sugar,
sifted, plus extra if needed

1–2 tablespoons milk

a few drops of vanilla extract

1. Preheat the oven to 300°F. Line three large baking sheets with nonstick parchment paper.

2. Put the sifted confectioners' sugar, almonds, and three-quarters of the egg whites into a large mixing bowl and mix to a paste, using a wooden spoon.

3. Put the superfine sugar and water into a small, heavy saucepan. Heat gently for 5 minutes, until the sugar has dissolved, tilting the pan to mix the ingredients together. Increase the heat and boil rapidly for 12–15 minutes, or until the mixture reaches 240°F on a candy thermometer, turns syrupy, and thickens.

4. Whisk the remaining egg white in a large, clean mixing bowl until you have stiff, moist-looking peaks, then gradually whisk in the hot syrup until the mixure is shiny. Spoon this into the almond paste and stir together gently until the mixture becomes stiff and shiny again. Add the pink food coloring, then mix well.

5. Spoon the mixture into a pastry bag fitted with a ½-inch tip and pipe forty ¾-inch circles onto the prepared baking sheets, about ¾ inch apart. Let stand for 30 minutes, or until a skin forms. Bake in the preheated oven for 12–15 minutes, with the door slightly ajar, until firm.

6. For the buttercream, put the butter in a large mixing bowl and beat until soft. Add half the sifted confectioners' sugar and beat until smooth. Add the remaining confectioners' sugar, 1 tablespoon of the milk, and all the vanilla extract and beat until creamy. Add a little extra confectioners' sugar to thicken or milk to make it runnier, if needed. Spoon the mixture into a pastry bag fitted with a large star tip.

7. Transfer the macarons, still on their paper, to a wire rack. Let cool for 1–2 hours, then peel off the paper. Pipe a swirl of buttercream on each of half the macarons and top each with another macaron.

8. These can be stored without the buttercream in an airtight container in a cool, dry place for up to five days.

Mini ginger caramel cookies

Makes: 20
Prep: 1¼ hours
Cook: 30–35 minutes
Set: 1–2 hours

Dulce de leche — a thick caramel sauce — is available in jars at good supermarkets and delicatessens. You can use a chocolate spread instead, if you prefer.

1 teaspoon ground ginger

1 cup confectioners' sugar, sifted

1⅓ cups almond meal (ground almonds)

2 extra-large egg whites

½ cup superfine sugar

3 tablespoons water

⅔ cup dulce de leche (caramel sauce)

1. Preheat the oven to 300°F. Line three large baking sheets with nonstick parchment paper.

2. Put the ginger, sifted confectioners' sugar, almonds, and two-thirds of the egg whites into a large mixing bowl and mix to a paste, using a wooden spoon.

3. Put the superfine sugar and water into a small, heavy saucepan. Heat gently for 5 minutes, until the sugar has dissolved, tilting the pan to mix the ingredients together. Increase the heat and boil rapidly for 12–15 minutes, or until the mixture reaches 240°F on a candy thermometer, turns syrupy, and thickens.

4. Whisk the remaining egg white in a large, clean mixing bowl until you have stiff, moist-looking peaks, then gradually whisk in the hot syrup until the mixture is shiny. Spoon this into the almond paste and stir together gently until the mixture becomes stiff and shiny again.

5. Spoon the mixture into a pastry bag fitted with a ½-inch tip and pipe forty ¾-inch strips onto the prepared baking sheets, about ¾ inch apart. Let stand for 30 minutes, or until a skin forms. Bake in the preheated oven for 12–15 minutes, with the door slightly ajar, until firm.

6. Transfer the cookies, still on their paper, to a wire rack. Let cool for 1–2 hours, then peel off the paper. Drop a teaspoon of dulce de leche on each of half the cookies and top each with another cookie.

7. These can be stored without the dulce de leche in an airtight container in a cool, dry place for up to five days.

Iced citrus marzipan thins

Makes: 30
Prep: 25 minutes
Set: overnight

Originally from Aix-en-Provence in France, these easy-to-make after dinner treats are full of citrus and almond goodness.

2 cups almond meal (ground almonds)

1 cup superfine sugar

1 extra-large egg

a few drops of citrus extract

finely grated rind of ½ orange

FOR THE ICING

1⅔ cups confectioners' sugar, sifted, plus extra for dusting

juice of 1 lemon

1. Line an 8-inch square baking pan with nonstick parchment paper, snipping diagonally into the corners, then pressing the paper into the pan so that the bottom and sides are lined. Lightly dust a work surface with confectioners' sugar.

2. Put the almonds and superfine sugar into a mixing bowl and stir. Add the egg, citrus extract, and orange rind and mix, using your hands, to form a stiff paste.

3. Knead the marzipan briefly on the prepared work surface, then press it into the bottom of the prepared pan, using the back of a spoon, until even and smooth. Let set for 1 hour.

4. For the icing, put the sifted confectioners' sugar and lemon juice into a mixing bowl and stir until smooth, then spread evenly over the marzipan. Cover and let stand in a cool place, but not the refrigerator, to dry overnight.

5. Cut the iced marzipan into bite-size shapes of your choice, using a candy or cookie cutter. Store in an airtight container in the refrigerator for up to two days.

Index